AF772423

Trade and Transport Facilitation

An Audit Methodology

John Raven

The World Bank
Washington, D.C.

First printing April 2000

ISBN: 0-8213-4719-5

Photo credits (clockwise from top left): Ship at berth, Port of New York and New Jersey Authority; Kenya Railways, ABB Transportation Limited; Rural street in China, Curt Carnemark, World Bank; Rehabilitated Urban Roads in Accra, Ghana, Ian Heggie, World Bank.

John Raven is director general of the International Express Carriers Conference.

Library of Congress Cataloging-in-Publication Data

Raven, John, 1920–
Trade and transport facilitation : an audit methodology / John Raven.
p. cm.
ISBN 0-8213-4719-5
1. International trade—Auditing. 2. Transportation—Auditing. I. Title.

HF1379 .R385 2000
657'.45—dc21 00-035912

Contents

Foreword

Alleviating poverty through direct assistance to beneficiaries as well as economic growth is a prominent World Bank Group objective. For this strategy to succeed, all potential impediments hindering the competitiveness of export industries must be tackled and reduced to the largest possible extent. International trade performance and efficiency are essential components of overall success. And in this new economy of instant communication, where goods and services are increasingly negotiated, ordered and handled electronically, the main bottleneck in the economy is more than ever delivery, that is, transport and logistics.

National frontiers—ports, airports, road border-crossing points—impose on incoming and outgoing consignments a complex set of procedural requirements. Countries that ensure that these are met with the minimum cost and delay to legitimate cargo and with full regard to public interest controls enjoy many advantages. They attract direct foreign investors to establish importing, production and distribution facilities and so increase employment. They repress and reduce opportunities and incentives for official and commercial corruption. They minimize import prices and so inflation, and give exporters, especially small and medium sized companies, a fair opportunity, with reliable, rapid delivery and pared delivery prices in increasingly competitive world markets.

The World Bank Group has participated, along with other financing agencies and many client countries, in notable improvements to basic visible transport infrastructure, through a wide range of road, rail, port, and airport developments.

Those investments will never yield their full potential returns in international trade performance, however, without parallel advances in systematic improvement of the invisible infrastructure of information generation and exchange which underpins and controls every export and import movement.

Such an effort has to begin with a clear understanding of the special characteristics of each country, and, indeed, of each significant border entry and import point. This *Facilitation Audit Methodology* offers an analytical approach to such a perception. It reflects practical experience in a number of Bank missions and inquiries in a range of developing countries.

This publication has been provided by John Raven, Director General of the International Express Carrier's Conference, as a token of his organization's belief in the power of steadily increasing Bank and business partnership to bring the positive benefits of global trading and transport to the full international community, with special concern for the acute needs of more disadvantaged economies. We want to express to him our sincere thanks for this valuable contribution to the permanent cooperation the Bank wishes to entertain with the private sector.

This cooperation is finding new, very tangible expression in the Global Facilitation Partnership for Transportation and Trade, which the World Bank is launching to provide a focus and forum for all those in the public and private sectors, who want to bring about lasting, significant improvements in the invisible infrastructure of transport and trade in all interested Bank member countries.

The Facilitation Audit is provided as a tool for all those who may be required to identify facilitation problems and begin the process of prescribing and providing appropriate remedies.

We hope this will prove a useful guide for all those who wish to answer effectively the challenge posed to transport by the demanding requirements of international trade.

Marc H. Juhel
Senior Port Specialist
Transport Division
World Bank

Acronyms and Abbreviations

APEC	Asian-Pacific Economic Cooperation
ASEAN	Association of Southeast Asian Nations
ASYCUDA	Automated System for Customs Data
ATA Carnet Systems	Admission Temporaire/Temporary Admission Notebook System
cif	Cost, insurance, and freight
EDI	Electronic Data Interchange
EU	European Union
FIATA	Federation of Forwarding Agents Associations
fob	Free on board
GATT	General Agreement on Tariffs and Trade
IATA	International Air Transport Association
IBCC	International Bureau of Chambers of Commerce
ICC	International Chamber of Commerce
ICS	International Chamber of Shipping
IECC	International Express Carriers' Conference
IMF	International Monetary Fund
IMO	International Maritime Organization
IRU	International Road Traffic Union
MERCOSUR	Mercado Comun del America del Sur (South America Common Market)
PSI	Preshipment Inspection Agency
SADC	Southern African Development Community
SWIFT	Society for Worldwide Interbank Financial Telecommunication
TEUs	Twenty-foot Equivalent Units
TIR	Transport International Routier (International Road Transport)
UN EDIFACT	United Nations Electronic Data Interchange for Administration, Commerce and Transport
UNCTAD	United Nations Conference on Trade and Development
WCO	World Customs Organization
WTO	World Trade Organization

Introduction

This outline account of a Facilitation Audit procedure consists of:

- An explanatory introduction.
- A set of questionnaires designed to support and structure personal interviews.
- A note on the analysis and interpretation of the results of these interviews and suggestions for organizing practical remedial action.

The purpose of this Audit is to examine and evaluate difficulties and obstacles presented to the cross-frontier movement of a routine consignment and its associated payment.

Experience shows that these center on official and other authoritative procedures and related information flows. "Authoritative" procedures, apart from Customs, security and other governmental controls include banking requirements, particularly when these combine payment with credit or discounting services, pre-shipment inspection regimes, non-competitive transport systems, for example monopoly airlines or national shipping lines and quasi-monopolistic port operations.

Customs form the hard core of most procedural problems. Operational inefficiency and outdated regulations are often aggravated by dishonesty.

There may be other difficulties from rigid, complex exchange controls, but, over the last thirty years, the International Monetary Fund (IMF) and World Bank have greatly reduced these additional handicaps.

Payment systems, especially full-dress documentary credits, still slow modern transport systems to the leisurely pace of 19th century paper-based banking practices. There is hardly any competition between banks in this part of their business. Many consider it is more profitable to palliate chronic delays by issuing letters of indemnity than to strive to get the poor best out of an essentially outdated procedure.

Trading communities are often captive customers of their local port. Geographical constraints can be powerfully reinforced by limited access to key container services. State ownership, protected from competition, adds an extra dimension to operational inefficiency.

Even after almost 50 years of growth, there are a surprising number of countries which have failed to assimilate and exploit the full potential benefits of multi-modal, through transport systems. Customs procedures, there, are still adjusted to traditional port-to-port movement and freight-forwarders or others seeking to set up as through-transport providers may be unable to do so for lack of necessary legal status.

All these difficulties cast serious burdens on traders and carriers with direct access to maritime services. Land-locked developing countries, dependent on transit arrangements, can incur a range of additional costs and handicaps.

While designed primarily for use in World Bank operations the Audit could be applied in appropriate projects or inquiries by any lending, aid or government agency or consultant advisers, always provided that there is assured, free access to all levels of management in the official and commercial sectors brought under review.

In World Bank terms it should enable a typical Appraisal or Pre-appraisal mission, considering a trade development or structural adjustment loan, or a port, airport or border crossing point investment project, to assemble, in two or three weeks, all necessary information for a trade facilitation section in its back-to-the office report.

The sort of audit set out in this document cannot provide the depth or range of information essential to identify and guide remedial action. It is intended and has served, in practice, to offer a reasonably reliable assessment of the general nature and balance of gross difficulties. In crude terms it should show pretty accurately where most of the important facilitation bodies are buried and offer an initial signpost to the sort of skills needed for priority expert advice and action.

In addition to the respondent categories covered in this Audit, it may, in certain counties, be useful to make similar approaches to a national standards organization, Departments of Health and Agriculture, and any Export Permit Control Agency.

Questionnaires

These questionnaires are addressed to the:

- Forwarder/Agent/Broker/Multimodal Transport Operator.
- Exporter.
- Importer.
- Shipping Line.
- Road Carrier.
- Airline.
- Express Operator.
- Port.
- Airport.
- Border Crossing Point.
- Customs.
- Commercial Bank.
- Exchange Control/Central Bank.
- Pre-shipment Inspection Agency.
- Chamber of Commerce.
- Department of Trade/External Trade.

They are intended for use as a structured support for personal interviews. If answers are written down this should be done as unobtrusively as possible.

Some questions are put to a number of respondents, in order to provide corroboration or identify significant discrepancies.

It is important to plan interviews in the light of the best available advice and information on suitable respondents. A Bank mission can normally draw on considerable in-house knowledge and judgement. This can be supplemented by prior consultation with international organizations, including the World Customs Organization (WCO), International Air Transport Association (IATA), International Chamber of Shipping (ICS), International Chamber of Commerce (ICC), Federation of Forwarding Agents Associations (FIATA), International Road Traffic Union (IRU) and the International Express Carriers' Conference (IECC).

It is always useful if the persons interviewed are not only well-known in the national institutional network, but are also active in some relevant regional or international organizations.

Interviews should be one-to-one and informal. Precision is less important than credibility. The purpose of the audit is to provide reliable judgements rather than accurate statistics.

Each set of questions is prefaced by a short note on the role/responsibilities of the respondents concerned.

It is important to follow the suggested sequence of interviews. Starting with Customs, for example, before obtaining any previous idea of their efficiency from shippers and carriers, to guide the direction and detail of questioning, will be a largely wasted opportunity, and having to go back for a second time, possibly with a very evident change of approach, could be a serious embarrassment.

It may be helpful to talk to the Department of Trade, or its equivalent, and any export Promotion Agency, after forming a firm estimate of Customs performance.

Every effort should be made to conduct interviews in a language easily used by the respondents. The added presence of an interpreter adds undesirable formality and lengthens the time demands on those being interviewed. Customs, as the official agency most likely to be associated with a facilitation audit, may offer to provide an interpreter, but any Customs presence at interviews could inhibit frank replies from commercial people.

It should be possible to complete initial interviews within 10 working days. A rapid sifting of replies and supplementary interview material should throw up any areas of special doubt or disagreement. These could then be explored in greater depth and detail. Three weeks, in total, should suffice to produce an outline report with key recommendations for action.

Interviewers may often know the answer to some questions before posing them, but should ask them, just the same. Many opening queries are intended to offer the respondent an opportunity to set his or her own activities in a working environment. Questions which may be more direct and less welcome are placed later in each Questionnaire.

No attempt is made, in the Audit, to engage in systematic measurement. Some "measurement" indices are sought, but approximations are all that might reasonably be expected at many points. The Audit should, however, show clearly where detailed measurement and associated costings are most necessary. Defining the exact scope of these assessment processes will be an important part of the third stage remedial Action Plan referred to in the final pages of this document.

An important—indeed indispensable—element in every Audit should be personal observation of actual operations at Customs posts, in ports and airports and at border-crossing points and in traders and agents offices.

Are work places clean and reasonably tidy? How do agents and Customs officers mix? Is the Customs counter noisy and subject to a good deal of thrusting and pushing or is the atmosphere workmanlike and reasonably peaceful? Is there a defined and well observed practice which keeps agents and traders on their side of the Customs counter or do they penetrate into Customs offices? When duty payments are made, are there any supplementary cash flows to Customs officers?

Is there any visual evidence of irregular payments being distributed among staff? Are Customs signatures given in Customs offices or directly in the presence of the trader or agent? How far are premises equipped for likely extremes of temperature? What are the sanitary arrangements for staff and others? When documents are first presented to Customs what is the rough proportion of queries/rejections?

Documentation is especially relevant. Specimen sets of documents necessary for each procedure should be collected. The number of copies demanded should be noted. It is useful to know whether Customs, carriers, ports and other operators impose pre-printed forms or are ready to accept the equivalent documents produced, on plain paper, from a computer or copying process.

Computer installations should not be taken at face—or screen—value. Users should be asked to call up key programs and execute a few typical operations.

Visits to Customs posts may need two approaches—an initial unofficial survey with a friendly agent or trader and a formal appointment to see what happens behind the counter.

Agent, Forwarder, Customs Broker, and Multimodal Transport Operator

The "agent" may, in practice, cover any or all of these activities.

In many developing countries agents' fees are the only practicable means of meeting Customs demands for routine "presents" without corresponding entries in the principals' accounts. This is particularly important, given that companies based in the United States are criminally liable for collusion in bribery of public officials even when this takes place abroad.

Agents are often recruited from the ranks of Customs services, on retirement or at the prospect of some particularly attractive commercial opportunity. One practical result is that senior agents may well be more expert in Customs legislation and operations than most of the officers they have to deal with.

This can result in agents making a tacit common front with Customs, against the real interests of their clients. Conversely, Customs frequently confine timely circulation of changes in requirements to their agent contacts.

One unfortunate side-effect of such relationships is that to spare embarrassment to the agents concerned,

Customs may routinely require principals to appear in person to defend themselves in any but the most pedestrian dispute or irregularity. Such unpredictable calls to potentially protracted interrogations can play havoc with a small company in which management is in one or two hands and threats of often severe penalties attached to Customs offences force distraction from vital sales or distribution responsibilities.

One recent development in this general sector is the tendency for Customs experts to move into consultancy where they are particularly active in handling major valuation, classification or other disputes or differences.

In most developed economies these arrangements focus on large professional consultancy firms with a range of other advisory and analytical services. It is interesting that, in Eastern Europe, however, retired senior Customs officers are offering largely personal services of introduction, negotiation and representation. This could indicate that, in current administrative conditions there, exercise of influence over former colleagues is more valuable than professional advice.

Some questions offer special opportunities for widening the scope of discussion. Consideration of costs of compliance with Customs requirements, for example, may stimulate the respondent to move gradually from up-front compliance costs to dispute and delay costs and then to any routine "unofficial" charges and exceptional expectations of irregular payments. A direct, initial question on Customs behavior, on the other hand, might well produce nothing.

In selecting respondents, (at least one large and one small), it is sensible to include the Chairman of the national forwarders' association. FIATA can usually supply the relevant details.

Questions

1. How many clients have you for a) export b) import?
2. How many consignments do you handle daily/annually under each head?
3. What services do you offer your clients—contract negotiation, logistics, multimodal transport as principal, multimodal transport as agent, express delivery, payment arrangements with banks, Customs release and clearance as agent, Customs release and clearance as licensed broker, Customs disputes, exchange controls or others (specify)? Do any regulatory constraints restrict your range of activities?
4. What is your experience of Customs operational efficiency at a) ports, b) airports and c) road frontiers, d) rail frontiers and e) inland container depots?
5. Do you have difficulties related to exchange controls? If so of what nature?
6. What are the average times taken to clear your goods A) outward and B) inward at a) ports, b) airports, c) road frontiers, d) rail frontiers and e) inland container depots?
7. In what circumstances are these times seriously exceeded?
8. What is your impression of the cost/efficiency of a) domestic and b) foreign banks in dealing with documentary credits?
9. What is your impression of the cost/efficiency of domestic/foreign transport services?
10. What is your impression of the efficiency of multimodal—especially container—movements a) into, b) within and c) out of, the country?
11. What is your impression of the cost/efficiency of a) port and b) airport facilities?
12. Do you experience difficulty in obtaining official and/or commercial information necessary for your transaction? If so, under what heads?
13. What are your main uses of computer systems—internal office systems, services to clients, interchange with Customs, transport providers, ports, airports, banks, exchange controls, others (specify)?
14. Do you use a) the Internet b) EDI c) e-mail, satellite communications?
15. Are facilities for such uses satisfactory?
16. Do you use any of the FIATA standard transport documents? If so, which?
17. What proportion of your inward consignments are subject to physical inspection by Customs? Are these also subject to inspection by other control agencies?

18. Do you, or your principals, deal with Customs disputes? Do you regard the frequency of such disputes as normal or excessive?
19. Is there a review board for such disputes? If so, does it function efficiently?
20. If an import permit is required, how many government agencies are concerned? What is your experience of dealing with each of them?
21. Are transit operations particularly difficult in respect of a) bonds, b) carnets, c) documentation?

Exporter

Traditional "stand alone" export and import transactions are declining in proportion to the explosive growth of cross frontier transfers of materials, parts, components and semi-finished and finished products within integrated multinational operational systems.

There are important direct links between decisions on direct foreign investment in productive or processing facilities, and so employment, on the one hand, and the ability of the host country to offer rapid, reliable movement of essential inward as well as outward consignments, on the other.

Yet many politicians and commentators continue to support an outdated "export, good; import, bad" economic morality. This is particularly noticeable in developing countries, where "export promotion" is still seen as an activity that can be separated out from international trade as a whole, and should enjoy special privileges and preference.

It can often seem, from superficial evidence, that Customs treatment reflects this advantage, when, in fact, there are a range of hidden delays and complications.

When imported goods arrive they are met immediately with the hardest procedural test in their transactional life-cycle—formal Customs declaration.

The time taken to meet all the demands of this procedure, often aggravated by additional inefficiencies in the documentary credit checks, which have to precede release of the goods to the designated recipient, is directly reflected in measurable delay in the port or airport.

Export consignments, on the other hand, are often sent for shipment just a few hours before the vessel or aircraft is due to leave. The consignor, quite naturally, declines to expose his goods a moment longer than necessary to risks of intermediate loss or damage. He keeps them in hand, until he can be sure that all necessary Customs requirements have been, or can easily be, completed immediately prior to loading.

There will very often, however, be days of delay between the point at which the consignment is allocated, by the shipper, for export and the point at which he can be confident that its final passage to ship or plane will be relatively uneventful.

In the meantime he or she may need to have complied with exchange controls to secure foreign currency transport costs, made relevant requests for any associated import permit for eventual replacement of scarce material used in manufacture or processing, lodged claims for writing off this consignment against the total of any temporary importation license, obtained an often specious quality certificate and secured space on what may be very infrequent transport services.

All these operations will be hidden within his own works and office. Often they are regarded as almost inevitable and natural features of a process which may never be consciously identified as adding up to an export delay or complication.

This situation casts extra importance on pushing and pursuing, as well as posing, relevant questions.

Questions

1. What are your main export items?
2. What is your overall export value annually? What proportion is this of your total output?
3. What are your principal markets?
4. Do you use one or several forwarders?
5. Are you responsible for any transport arrangements? If so which?
6. What proportion of your shipments are containerized?
7. What means of transport do you use, and in what proportions (value), for the basic part of your international transport?

8. What are your usual selling terms—fob, cif, ex-works, delivered, and so on?
9. If you use documentary credits what is your impression of the efficiency/cost of this method of payment?
10. Do you have frequent difficulties in:
    - Customs clearance?
    - Exchange controls?
11. If so, what sort?
12. Are you concerned directly with ports/airports of shipment? If so what is your impression of their cost/efficiency?
13. Do you experience difficulty in obtaining official or commercial information needed in your transactions.? If so under what heads?
14. If a pre-shipmeny inspection regime is in force what are its main components? Is the result effective in terms of presumed objectives? What additional complications, costs and delays, if any, does it cast on traders and carriers? What would be preferable alternatives?
15. Do you have communication problems within or to and from your country? If so, under what heads?
16. If you have queries on official requirements, at home or abroad, do you go to:
    - Chamber of Commerce?
    - Trade Association (if so, which?)?
    - Customs?
    - Other government department or agency (if so, which?)?
17. Do you participate in any official export promotion activities? If so, which and how useful are they?
18. What are your main uses of computer systems—internal office systems, services to clients, interchange with Customs, transport providers, ports, airports, banks, exchange controls, others (specify)?
19. What are your main means of communication—post, telephone, express delivery, fax, EDI, Internet, satellite. . . ?
20. Do you have difficulties in using any of these communication methods? If so, in what respects?
21. What proportion of your inward consignments are subject to physical inspection by Customs? Are these consignments also subject to inspection by other control agencies?
22. Do you or your agent deal with Customs disputes? Do you regard the frequency of such disputes as normal or excessive?
23. Do you have frequent recourse to Certificates of Origin? What is your experience of the issue and use of these documents?.
24. What is your experience of drawback or export refund procedures?

Importer

It is useful to cover:

- A local importer of goods for home use.
- A local importer engaged in electronic assembly or garment make-up, with consequent reliance on temporary importation or drawback.
- A "foreign" multinational company importing for the home market and/or re-export after processing.

The multinational importer should be able to offer comparative judgements of conditions in other developing or developed countries which might be less familiar to local companies. Such companies are also especially familiar with large computer systems. It is always interesting to know to what extent such capabilities are able to interface with local requirements, especially those of Customs, port, airport, banking and transport services.

It is important to acquire a general sense of the political and official status of importing. Does it need to be able to prove some necessary relationship to exports to make a facilitation case to government?

Clearly, carriers welcome business, regardless of direction, and agents may well prefer import transactions, because they normally encounter more difficulties, and, therefore, generate larger fees than exports. On the other hand "export promotion" is still institutionalized, under that name, in many developing countries and has only recently given place to "trade development" in many lending and aid programs.

Questions

1. What are your main import items?
2. What is the annual overall value and volume of your import operations?
3. What are your principal source countries?
4. Do you use one or several import agents/ Customs brokers?
5. What are your usual buying terms—fob, cif, ex-works, delivered, and so on?
6. What proportion of your imports, by value, are containerized?
7. Are these mainly in groupage or full container loads? How many full container loads do you receive annually?
8. Where are containers:
   - Cleared through Customs?
   - Opened and emptied?
9. If you use documentary credits what is your impression of their cost/efficiency?
10. Do you have regular, significant difficulties in:
    - Customs clearance
    - Exchange control?

    If so what sort?
11. Do you have direct contacts with ports and airports of entry? If so what is your impression of their cost/efficiency?
12. What proportion of your imports enter the country by road or rail? Do you have special difficulties in respect of:
    - Customs clearance at the frontier?
    - Other official controls on goods, vehicles and drivers?

    If so, what sort?
13. In seeking official/commercial information needed for your import business do you approach:
    - Customs?
    - Chamber of Commerce?
    - Trade association—if so which?
    - Other government departments—if so which?
    - UNCTAD Trade Points, if any?
    - The Internet?
14. Do you have any problems in obtaining such information? If so, what sort of information and what sort of problems?
15. Do you have communication problems within the country? If so, of what sort?
16. How do you use computer systems in your own business? How far, if at all, do you use these to interface, automatically, with Customs, carriers banks and other services?

Carriers

Carriers, with the possible exception of integrated express operators—a relatively minor sector in most developing economies—are still most conveniently handled under separate modal headings.

Maritime transport will be the usual front-runner, with special importance attaching to road and rail movements for countries served by or serving transit operations.

For many years, traders in numerous developing countries had to depend on national shipping lines, often protected by virtual monopoly status and confronted by equally monolithic and bureaucratic central chartering agencies, sometimes disguised as Shippers' Councils. Privatization, very usefully encouraged by the IMF and World Bank, has reduced these commercial handicaps, but all too frequently a public monopoly has just slid, sideways, into a quasi-cartel agreement with selected "independent" partners.

Such arrangements have done little to force carriers to meet and anticipate client requirements, maintain modern computer and communication systems and play a fully influential part in moves toward Customs modernization and reform.

The assimilation of containerized through movement is still a problem in many countries. It is even more difficult to move from passive assimilation to positive exploitation. Major obstacles include gross inefficiencies at functional interfaces; the use of Customs and other official control procedures designed for port-to-port movements; uncertainty whether to treat the container itself as an import item or a means of transport, and delays in adjusting legal, fiscal and exchange control requirements to the unfamiliar requirements and status of the multimodal transport operator.

In countries where conditions inhibit or frustrate locally based multimodal transport operators, traders have to depend on the advice and services of foreign, usually multinational agencies, with consequent difficulties of communication and an extra strain on scarce currencies.

Transit is a key factor in the economic and social stability of a number of developing land-locked countries. It is doubtful if their specific needs would weigh very largely in the balance of opinion or priority in countries of maritime access, if it were not for a gradually broadening area of transport and port privatization and associated competition. In some access countries political pressures can constrain the scope and efficiency of facilities for neighboring land-locked economies.

The Bank and IMF, with obligations to a wide range of clients, are in a unique position to assess and, possibly improve, those aspects of transit systems which may be largely inaccessible to direct influence from land-locked governments themselves. This Audit includes questions designed to assist preliminary fact-gathering for this purpose.

Recent UNCTAD Expert Meetings have demonstrated the importance of Customs requirements and efficiency in the operation and costs of transit systems through, and to and from land-locked developing countries.

It is no part of the purpose of the Audit to deal with, or inquire into, physical infrastructural resources. Nevertheless, though its immediate concern is with the invisible infrastructure, in the form of procedural constraints, all procedures depend on the submission or exchange of information, and the means of processing and transmitting that information are very relevant to overall efficiency.

In containerized traffic, moreover, the number of consignments to be cleared can build up more rapidly than the means available to process associated information. This may produce pressures to move that processing to points outside and separate from ports and airports.

Dry ports or inland container terminals are typical examples of facilities that, perhaps seen initially as expedients, can often become a valid part of the long-term transport infrastructure. There are important procedural overtones and the Audit touches on these here and in the sections on ports, airports and border-crossing points.

The maritime Bill of Lading, with the obligations it casts on the carrier, can often contribute to procedural delays, especially when the Bill figures in documentary credit requirements. Air transport has special significance for land locked countries and countries with very large land masses and poor surface communications.

Express delivery services, using a basic air transport component, are now an essential ingredient in implementing time-sensitive conventional international transactions and supporting the growing proportion—already between one third and one half of global trade in goods—that is represented by the cross-border movement of components, semi-processed and finished products and spare parts within integrated in-company supply, production and distribution systems.

The very limited timeframes within which such services must deliver consignments, in order to justify their charges and so ensure return on their worldwide investments in aircraft, road vehicles, support staff and communication systems, place these operators and their representative trade bodies among the most active advocates of trade facilitation.

As they cannot function effectively, and so profitably, in countries where Customs are inefficient and dishonest, they may well be inactive or represented only by local agents, for relatively time-insensitive deliveries in many countries covered by this type of audit.

For that reason, while there is a short Questionnaire addressed specifically to these operators, a number of questions bearing on the express delivery function have been inserted at other points in the Audit document.

Rail operators, particularly important in transit regimes, tend to view compliance with Customs and other official requirements as an exercise in cooperation with the inevitable. They tend to concentrate their attention on managing the transport system itself, with only marginal attention to the largely separate life-cycle of the international freight consignment.

Questions for Shipping Line

1. What volume of cargo do you handle a) inward and b) outward annually?
2. How many TEUs do you handle a) inward and b) outward annually?
3. What are the main countries of a) origin and b) destination?
5. Do you use/issue IMO standard manifests or International Chamber of Commerce standard bills of lading and/or non-negotiable sea waybills? If not would you be prepared to adopt such documents? Do your government agencies accept them?
6. How do you move manifest information—by post, express carrier, in ship's bag, fax, EDI?
7. Do you experience serious delays or obstacles in any of these operations? If so, under what heads?
8. Do you experience serious delays by importers in presenting bills of lading? If so, do you know why?
9. What is your cargo loss/damage experience in national ports?
10. Have you automated your internal operations and communications between head office and branches? If so, under what main heads?
11. Do you exchange data electronically with Customs to meet their import/export requirements? If so, what is your experience of the efficiency of these arrangements?
12. Do you exchange data electronically with other entities—customers, banks, ports . . .? If so, which?
13. What is your impression of the efficiency of a) ports b) Customs?
14. Do you operate inland container collection and delivery services? If not, why?
15. Do you use a) the Internet b) satellite communication? If so for what purposes?

Questions for Road Carrier

1. What volume of a) containerized and b) non-containerized cargo do you handle a) inward and b) outward annually?
2. What proportions do the total of these movements bear to your overall operations?
3. What are the main countries of a) origin and b) destination for your international consignments?
4. Do you operate any international door-to-door services?
5. Do you operate TIR or ATA procedures. If so, are there any special difficulties? If not, why not?
6. What are your main ports of entry and exit? What is your experience of their efficiency, cost and security standards?
7. What is your experience of Customs at a) land frontiers and b) ports for a)inward and b) outward movements? What is the average time for release of the goods by Customs under each of these four heads?
8. Do you use inland container terminals/dry ports? If so, what is your experience of cost/efficiency?
9. In which foreign country do you experience most difficulties with Customs or other control agencies—immigration, vehicle requirements, phytosanitary inspection. . . ?
10. Which parts of your transport functions are automated?
11. Do you exchange data electronically with other business and official entities? If so, which?
12. Do you receive adequate and timely information of Customs and other official requirements?
13. If you need information on Customs and other procedures in foreign countries where do you go for help?
14. What are your main means of communication—post, telephone, express delivery, fax, EDI, Internet. . . ?
15. Do you have difficulties in using any of these communication methods? If so, in what respects?
16. In transit operations do you have particular difficulty in respect of a) designated routes, b) Customs escorts, c) bonds and d) documentation.

Questions for Airline

1. What is the a) volume b) value of your a) export and b) import cargo annually?

2. What are the main countries of a) origin and b) destination?
3. What is the average/usual airport dwell-time of your cargo for a) export and b) import?
4. Do you operate express delivery door-to-door services?
5. How do you move controlling information—waybills and manifests—with pilot, fax, EDI, Internet, other?
6. Do you exchange data electronically? If so with whom?
7. Do you operate feeder road services?
8. Do you have serious difficulties with:
   - Customs?
   - Exchange control?
   - Security?
   - Pre-shipment inspection?
   - Other official agencies?

   If so, of what sort?
9. Is airfreight able to exploit its full inherent advantages—speed, light packing, security—in import/export traffic? If not, what are the main disincentives and obstacles?

Questions for Express Carrier

1. Are you part of an internationally integrated carrier or operating on an independent national/regional base?
2. How many a) export and b) import consignments do you declare to Customs annually? What is the total value at a) export and b) import?
3. What time is usually required to pass a) documents, b) non-dutiable or de minimis goods and c) dutiable goods through airports for a) export and b) import?
4. Would you be able to extend your services if these times were reduced? If so in what respects?
5. What do you identify as the main causes of delay—Customs, security, airport procedures/facilities, compulsory warehousing, pre-shipment inspection. . . ?
6. Is your business constrained by a) a postal monopoly, b) a licensing system, c) special charges or fees? If so, in what respects?

Ports

Ports are focal points for almost the full range of facilitation difficulties. In particular the efficiency, even timing, of many of their operations, is strongly influenced, if not dictated, by Customs.

Customs hours of attendance, for example, place strict limits on port working. Any approximation to comprehensive inspection of cargo, especially containerized cargo, throws substantial tasks and costs on port management.

Finding containers, moving them to the Customs area for inspection, dealing with the frequent physical aftermath of such inspections, returning the container to stack or quay and recording any consequences, can add substantially to the already sufficient problems of developing country port operators and take up as much as half the availability of such key equipment as lifting and moving appliances.

There are often serious deficiencies in port management itself. There are still ports that receive cargo without specifying the presentation of a Standard Shipping Note or equivalent EDI message, which has been found invaluable in modern port practice. It is frequently impossible to obtain a written, accurate account of the main port procedures. Delays fixed by regulations for acceptance of responsibility for cargo in shed or on the quay are often unreasonably long, which, with associated extra risks of damage and pilferage, add to the daily irritations of port users and inflate insurance premiums.

Ports usually provide the most accessible and reliable source of information on delays and inefficiencies in the international trade transaction.

Their principal customers—shipowners—can cover a very wide range of sizes and capabilities. Global maritime and nonvessel-owning container operators will be able to provide excellent data, produced from high-quality automated recording, processing and communication systems. At the other end of the resource scale Customs will have to accommodate small, single-vessel owners, scarcely able to complete simple forms correctly, and often with strong inclinations to confuse trading with smuggling.

Chronic delays in ports, attributable to lax or over-rigid banking practices, are common for goods subject to payment by documentary credit. In countries with heavy duty rates or fluctuating exchange rates and control systems small importers often refuse or are unable to meet the requirements which will permit them to secure release from the shipowner or Customs.

In some ports logistics and warehousing rates make it convenient to let goods stay in the port rather than move to inland storage.

Most ports of any consequence are the focus for significant trading communities—exporters, importers, forwarding and Customs agents, banks, insurers and shipping and other transport companies. They focus relatively substantial Customs staffs, accustomed to being in daily contact with business operators.

A surprising number of ports, even those with poor management standards and performance, bring much needed and very valuable cohesion to these local business communities, through port consultative committees, on either a stand alone basis or in cooperation with a Chamber of Commerce or other trade body. These committees are often the only mechanism for regular consultation between trade and Customs.

Shipping and container economics have, inevitably, reduced the number of principal ports at which direct international liner services are available. In choosing these ports, shipowners will give close attention to experience in rapid turn-round for vessels, customer satisfaction, damage, loss and pilferage experience, and standards of official integrity.

Few ports in developing countries are following the lead of major international counterparts in establishing communication networks with other ports along the lines of their main traffic flows. Such links can pass very valuable information on vessel characteristics, requirements and defects, well ahead of the arrival of ships and cargo.

Questions

1. What is the tonnage/value of general merchandise handled annually for a) import and b) export?
2. How many a) export and b) import TEUs are handled annually?
3. Which overseas ports are your main trading partners? Do you have any cooperative arrangement with any of them? If so, of what sort?
4. What is the average dwell time, in the port, at a) export and b) import for a) general cargo, b) containers and c) roll-on/roll-off vehicles?
5. What are the main causes of undue delays under all these heads—Customs, late arrival/presentation of manifests/bills of lading, banking requirements under payment terms, unavailability of connecting transport, exchange controls, preshipment inspection, tardy take-up by consignees. . . ?
6. Do you require a standard shipping note, or an equivalent EDI message, as a condition of receiving export cargo?
7. Do you have a generally available, up-to-date written account of the main port procedures of concern to commercial users and official agencies?
8. Do you use computers to handle any port procedures for a) containerized or b) general cargo? If so, which?
9. Are you exchanging, or planning to exchange data, electronically?. If so, with whom?
10. Do you have a port consultative committee? If so what is its composition and scope?
11. What services do you perform, and what facilities do you provide, for a) Customs and b) any other official agency? What are the rough costs and main consequences? Are you repaid or compensated in any way?
12. At what stage of movement do you first accept responsibility in respect of cargo on your premises?
13. What are the number of Customs officers employed in the port?
14. What are their normal working hours and what provisions are made for extended working? What are the customary overtime rates?
15. What proportion of consignments—in very general terms—are presented by a) traders in person, b) agents c) carriers—for example, truck drivers or shipboard staff?

16. What is the quality of cooperation between Customs and other control agencies dealing with goods and means of transport?
17. Are Customs entrusted with other controls, such as phytosanitary or security checks? If not how, in terms of efficiency and effectiveness are such formalities, if any, applied?
18. Is the bulk of the Customs procedure managed within Customs or is the declarant or his agent obliged to take the documents from one officer to another for a series of separate checks?
19. How many signatures are required in the entire process of Customs clearance?
20. Is there a written, freely available and well-publicized account of the procedures necessary to move goods and vehicles efficiently through the port and Customs systems? Procedures?
21. What computer and associated equipment is used by port management and what are its main applications?
22. To what extent are users able to communicate directly, computer to computer, with the port. Are any EDI messages, for this purpose, based on the international UN EDIFACT standards?
23. What is the rough proportion of declarations for which supporting documents—invoices, certificates of origin, waybills, bills of lading, and so on—are inspected?
24. What is the rough proportion of consignments/containers which are physically inspected.
25. What is the quality and nature of container inspection?
26. If inspection is superficial, what purpose is said to be served?
27. What is the incidence (rough percentage of total declarations) of procedural difficulties and disputes, and what are the principal causes—classification, value, suspicion of contraband and so on?
28. Are goods and vehicles delayed while all such differences are resolved or are some issues recorded for later resolution, while the goods are released for onward movement?
29. What is the experience of pilferage and loss—good, bad average—for a) general merchandise and b) containerized cargo while still in Customs custody?

Airports

At airports the number of carriers will be very limited and all will be accustomed to computerized operations and the use of uniquely numbered, internationally standard, non-negotiable air waybills.

For freight carried on passenger flights, IATA, to which most major airlines belong, has schooled its members to depend on authorized agents for all stages of cargo handling after unloading, including, in particular, Customs clearance. These agents are often of markedly higher quality than their counterparts in ports and at border crossing points.

As the key transport document—the air waybill—is non-negotiable, it cannot form the basis of full-dress documentary credit procedures and consignments are delivered directly to the person named in the bill. Customs formalities tend, therefore, to be the main factor in release times.

Customs handling consignments at airports will work almost entirely with reasonably experienced and "professional" agents and may often be largely insulated from the general trading community. Unfortunately, there are still numerous countries in which procedures for dealing with air freight are still ad hoc adaptations of classical seaport practices.

Express operations, in the hands of major global companies, have tended to run, ahead of conventional airfreight in Customs practice.

The World Customs Organization has produced a standard set of Express Guidelines, under which express consignments are given immediate release, provided prescribed control data has been submitted to Customs, from audited computer systems at specified periods in advance of aircraft arrival.

The degree to which airport management can give useful input to the Audit will depend on the nature of their operations.

Some may operate obligatory warehouses, through which even express consignments, and may constrain air carriers to use a monopoly ground service. Security is a special and legitimate concern for air movements, but all-cargo flights should be less cumbered with these regulations than passenger carrying aircraft.

Customs procedures often vary between port and airport. When this happens the re is a strong likelihood that the airport procedures will be simpler, and this could provide useful arguments and precedents in looking for easier port treatment. One contributory reason, however, may be absence any delays connected with documentary credits, as the air waybill is a non-negotiable document and the carrier or his agent just delivers consignments to the person named on the bill.

Some of the following questions will be addressed directly to airport managers. Others will need on-site ad hoc contact with agents, Customs and carriers.

Questions

1. What are the rough orders of magnitude for annual value (ascertained from declarations) and tonnage for a) import, b) export and c) transit consignments?
2. What are the average delay times—from arrival to departure—for a) imports, b) exports, c) transit consignments of a) conventional airfreight and b) express deliveries?
3. What are the total number of Customs staff?
4. What are the normal hours/days of Customs attendance? What provisions are made for extended working? What are the customary overtime rates?
5. What proportion of consignments—in very general terms—are presented by a) consignors/consignees in person, b) agents c) carriers—for example, truck drivers, airlines?
6. What is the quality of cooperation between Customs and other control agencies dealing with goods and means of transport?
7. Are Customs entrusted with other controls, such as phytosanitary or security checks? If not how, in terms of efficiency and effectiveness are such formalities, if any, applied?
8. Are Customs entrusted with immigration checks or, if not, do immigration staff work in reasonable cooperation with Customs?
9. What are the principal security regulations applied air cargo? Do these differ between consignments carried in holds of passenger aircraft and all-cargo flights?
10. Is there a written, freely available and well-publicized account of the procedures necessary to move goods efficiently through the airport, in accordance with Customs and other control procedures?
11. What computer and associated equipment is available and what are its main applications?
12. What is the quality of any software used for processing Customs formalities and of the operational skills available to use it?
13. To what extent are traders/agents/carriers able to communicate directly, computer to computer, with Customs. Are any EDI messages based on the international UN EDIFACT standards?
14. What is the rough proportion of declarations for which supporting documents—invoices, certificates of origin, waybills, bills of laning, and so on—are inspected?
15. What is the rough proportion of consignments which are physically inspected.
16. What is the incidence (rough percentage of total declarations) of procedural difficulties and disputes, and what are the principal causes—classification, value, suspicion of contraband, and so on?
17. Are goods and vehicles delayed while all such differences are resolved or are some issues recorded for later resolution, while the goods are released for onward movement?
18. What is the experience of pilferage and loss—good, bad average—for goods while on airport premises?

Border Crossing Points

These can offer a very difficult procedural environment.

The road transport industry, worldwide, is highly fragmented. Borders bring together a mass of small, local carriers with a mix of major regional or fully international road operators and some distributive arms of large manufacturing companies. Some arrivals will bring standard computerized print-out documents, others may only provide hand-written papers of dubious authenticity. Customs cannot apply any single set of procedures which can deal effectively and speedily with all these types of declarant.

Furthermore the key figure, for Customs purposes, is the truck driver, who may be completely or very largely ignorant of the characteristics and background of the load he happens to be carrying.

If a well-informed agent is on hand then processing may be easier. Unfortunately, at most borders in developing countries, an uncomfortably large number of consignments arrive with little more than basic, often badly prepared documentation to cover goods, vehicle and driver. All these have to be dealt with together, in contrast to the position at ports and airports, where goods can be cleared quite separately from vessels/aircraft and crews.

The physical conditions and restricted range of Customs management levels at typical border crossing points tends to encourage systematic corruption. Large bribes for serious dereliction of duty, with grave social consequences in respect, for example of illicit drugs, arms or unidentified nuclear substances, are masked by a background of relatively innocuous routine "facilitation" payments.

An additional feature of border crossings is the physical proximity of two separate national Customs services, handling export and import formalities. For ports and airports, these services may be thousands of miles apart. At land borders they are usually within hailing distance. It is common sense, and modern Customs practice, to encourage them to co-ordinate their functions to facilitate rapid clearance of consignments through both sets of controls.

Finally facilities—electricity supply, computers, telephone lines—which are taken for granted at ports and airports, may all be unavailable or unreliable at land borders.

Questions

1. What are the rough orders of magnitude for annual value (ascertained from declarations) and volume (number of vessels, containers, roll-on/roll-off loads, consignments) processed by Customs?
2. What is the relative importance of transit consignments and imports for home consumption?
3. What is the number and value of TIR and ATA Carnets handled annually?
4. What are the average delay times—from arrival to departure—at the border?
5. What are the number of Customs officers employed? What provisions are made for extended working? What are the customary overtime rates?
6. What is the quality of cooperation between Customs and other control agencies dealing with goods and means of transport?
7. Are Customs entrusted with other controls, such as phytosanitary or security checks? If not how, in terms of efficiency and effectiveness are such formalities, if any, applied?
8. Is there any cooperation, at the border, between adjacent export and import Customs services? If so, under what heads?
9. Is the bulk of the Customs procedure managed within Customs or is the declarant or his agent obliged to take the documents from one officer to another for a series of separate checks?
10. How many signatures are required in the entire process of Customs clearance?
11. Is there a written, freely available and well-publicized account of the procedures necessary to move goods and the vehicle efficiently through Customs and other official requirements?
12. What computer and associated equipment is available and what are its main applications?
13. What communication facilities are available to a) Customs, b) drivers and c) agents?
14. How is the post equipped to deal with likely extremes of temperature?
15. Is there reliable electricuity supply?
16. What is the rough proportion of declarations for which supporting documents—invoices, certificates of origin, waybills, and so on—are inspected?
17. What is the rough proportion of consignments/containers that are physically inspected.

18. Are additional formalities for driver-accompanied vehicles, including road-worthiness and weight certificates, and driving license, passport and visas, carried out simultaneously with controls on the goods, or in separate sequence?
19. How far do these secondary requirements contribute to the total processing time?
20. What is the quality and nature of container inspection?
21. What is the incidence (rough percentage of total declarations) of procedural difficulties and disputes, and what are the principal causes—classification, value, suspicion of contraband, and so on?
22. Are goods and vehicles delayed while all such differences are resolved or are some issues recorded for later resolution, while the goods are released for onward movement?
23. What is the experience of pilferage and loss—good, bad average—for consignments while still in Customs custody?

Commercial Banks

The conventional trade transaction requires that while goods move from seller to buyer, payment should be pass in the reverse direction.

The immense expansion of world trade, following and fuelling the Industrial Revolution linked buyers and sellers across great distances, many weeks, if not months, distant by any known means of communication.

In that situation banks, in cooperation with finance houses and merchants, devised a remarkable payment system—the documentary credit—that enabled the seller to be sure that his goods could not pass to the buyer until due payment had been made, while the buyer knew that his money would not pass to the seller until the goods were safely in hand.

In its most efficient period, toward the end of the nineteenth century, this system operated on the basis of key documents of title, carried by international mail services operating far faster than ordinary cargo movements.

Because of continuing, if generally diminished—exchange risks in certain economies and the commercial uncertainties of casual or novel trading relationships, the documentary credit is still a familiar feature of international trade for many developing countries.

Unfortunately the increasing efficiency of world transport networks and the failings of numerous postal services have combined to produce often significant delays to goods at import, pending the arrival and bank processing of the documents needed to authorize their release to the buyer or his agent.

There is practically no competition between banks to improve this position and user pressures are severely limited because many documentary credit customers also depend on their bank for other credit arrangements.

The International Chamber of Commerce, which sets the broad rules for documentary credit practices, is currently considering an electronic alternative or equivalent to the traditional paper-based procedures, but progress is slow and the overall credit system has a very low priority in most banking strategies.

The practical result is chronic delays at import, particularly of containerized cargo with special complications for groupage container loads of which only part are subject to these credit arrangements.

Such delays are cited, in self-exculpation by ports and Customs, to distract attention from or, at least, dilute, their own inefficiencies.

The banks earn extra fees by releasing goods to supposed consignees on the basis of guarantees contained in letters of so-called "indemnity."

These are an unsatisfactory expedient because they cannot, in fact, cover unassessable contingent obligations to third parties. Furthermore they are expensive—so enabling banks to make additional profits from their own inadequacies—and limited in scope, being available, normally, only to favored customers of unimpeachable status.

It is extremely unlikely that banks, when interviewed, will express anything but satisfaction with the "normal" functioning of the documentary credit system. Traders and agents are likely to be very circumspect and some other participants not at all familiar with the problem.

Ports and shipowners are the most reliable source of factual information.

Questions

1. What is the approximate a) number b) value of documentary credits on a) export b) import consignments, handled by you annually?
2. Are documentary credits the normal method of payment for your customers at a) import and b) export? If no what are the other, preferred payment systems in each direction?
3. Do you observe ICC Standard Rules for Documentary Credits? Does a national representative attend meetings of the ICC Banking Commission?
4. Are you linked to SWIFT? If so, for what purposes?
5. Do your clients have difficulties in managing exchange requirements? If so, of what sort and how might these problems be reduced?
6. Do you have significant dealings with Customs? If so, for what purposes, and how far are you satisfied with the way in which these are managed?
7. What proportion of initial applications for payment under a documentary credit are you obliged to reject? What are the most frequent reasons?
8. Do you issue letters of indemnity to cover late arrival of documents? Is this a common or exceptional practice? Can any customers secure such cover? What is the basis of charging for this service?
9. How do you normally receive documents from overseas correspondent banks, in documentary credit operations—ordinary post, express post, private express companies. . . ?
10. Do you exchange any import or export data electronically? If so, with whom and for what purpose?
11. Do you experience frequent delays in receipt of such documents? Do you record these and analyze their causes? What, in your opinion, are the main reasons—customer error, pace of processing by overseas banks, physical transmission problems?

Exchange Control Authorities

Exchange control restrictions now play a limited role in the practical procedural chain affecting goods in international movement.

Up until thirty years ago the situation, in the wake of the second World War and the withdrawal of external backing for many national currencies, following political independence, was very different. Maximizing the inward flow of scarce hard currencies became acquired high fiscal and economic priority, so that checking the accuracy of export invoicing and curbing expenditure on external services, including transport, was a major administrative function.

Decades of IMF and World Bank influence toward trade liberalization, the development of more open political attitudes toward external trading, coupled with the necessarily temporary expedient of replacing certain inefficient Customs controls with the services of specialist private agencies, have reduced these constraining pressures, but certain countries, including those in the latest wave of emerging independent states, are still obliged to apply rules of varying scope and severity.

The usual instrument for managing exchange controls is either direct intervention by the Central bank, delegation to a specialized Exchange Control Agency or management, under stipulated rules, by commercial banks.

Questions

1. What are the main objectives of your current exchange controls in relation to international trade and transport?
2. How are such controls applied in practice—by a single national agency, through a number of offices in commercial centers, through commercial banks. . . ?
3. Do you consult trade, transport and banking interests a) formally and/or b) informally? If so by what means, and on what aspects of control?

4. What is the role of Customs, if any, in applying your controls?
5. Is there a clearly defined, written and generally available set of exchange control regulations? How are changes notified to traders and banks?
6. How are innocent infringements handled? How is guilt established? Who tries cases and hears appeals?
7. Would a dispute normally have any effect on the movement of the goods concerned?
8. Do your documentary requirements include negotiable bills of lading for maritime shipments? If so what do you do for air consignments?
9. What, if any, are your relations with pre-shipment inspection agencies?

Customs

Customs are invariably found at the core of any significant set of international trade facilitation problems.

In many countries, they are not only a major cause of cost and delay, in themselves , but also furnish a convenient screen, behind which many other participants can attach their own inefficiencies. Quoted by traders, agents, carriers and ports as the principal, if not sole, cause of all border-crossing problems, Customs tend to furnish, often unwittingly, an unreasonable excuse for many failings at other points in the life-cycle of the international trade transaction.

For this reason, while it is desirable to place Customs well down the sequence of interviews, so that they can be interviewed in the light of previously expressed user opinions, they may well offer additional information and assessments that could justify some short second stage discussion with some other participants.

The answers to several questions put to Customs may already be known as the result of earlier interviews. These questions should be put just the same, as any substantial difference in Customs/trade perception could, in itself, be significant.

The Questionnaire cannot cover more than a few of the many aspects of Customs practice and procedure that influence the efficiency and cost of an international trade transaction. A much wider view of these can be had from the International Chamber of Commerce Customs Guidelines. The facilitation benefits of certain key procedural reforms are described, in even greater detail, in the Guidelines to the revised World Customs Organization Kyoto Convention. Possible delay causes are usefully set out in the WCO Time Required for Release Study

Any in-office interview to process the Questionnaire should be supplemented by visits to Customs posts at aport, airport and border crossing point.

Basic information on member administrations and names of suitable contacts can usually be had from the World Customs Organization.

Some of the following questions also figure among those to be asked at Customs posts handling port, airport and border crossing operations. Any variation in the answers will be particularly interesting.

Questions

1. How many a) export b) import declarations and c) transit operations are handled annually?
2. What is the total value of consignments covered by these declarations?
3. What proportion of government revenue is represented by Customs duties/taxes on international consignments?
4. What is the total number of staff employed in the service?
5. What is the average time from submission of the import entry to release of goods from your custody, in maritime trade for a) conventional general merchandise b) containerized cargo and c) roll-on/roll-off vehicles at a) export and b) import?
6. What are the corresponding times for road-borne consignments at main land frontier posts at a) export b) imports?
7. What are the corresponding times for airfreight consignments of a) documents b) non dutiable and de minimis and c) dutiable, goods?
8. Are the times in 5, 6 and 7 static or decreasing?
9. Do you consider any of these release times unsatisfactory and if so which? What do you see as the main causes?

10. Do you separate procedures and documentation to give "release" of goods from physical controls from those for "clearance" of the transaction following the satisfaction of fiscal requirements?
11. Are your paper forms aligned on the UN standard documentary system?
12. Are you using or planning to use computers in any operations? If so which? Do/will these include direct data exchanges? If so, with whom? Do you use UN/EDIFACT messages?
13. Do you use/plan to use ASYCUDA or any other proprietary Customs system? If so which? Are you satisfied with a) the product, b) post-implementation support and c) technological top-up?
14. Do you send delegates to WCO technical committees? If so, which?
15. How many disputes are lodged with/recorded by Customs annually? What is the largest single focus of difference—valuation, classification, temporary importation compliance. . .?
16. Have you an up to date, generally available Customs Code? Do you circulate public notices of changes and interpretations?
17. Do you carry out post-entry audits? If so who is responsible for the work?
18. Do you have an active Customs/Trade Consultative Committee?
19. Do you implement a) the GATT Valuation Code and b) the WCO Harmonised System?
20. Do you operate TIR and ATA procedures?
21. What services/facilities do you provide for other government agencies in connection with international trade consignments?
22. What services/facilities do you require at a) ports and b) airports? Do you pay for any of these? If so, which?
23. What proportion of a) conventional consignments b) containers are inspected at import?
24. Where do you normally inspect containers? How do you select for inspection? What are the main features of such inspection?
25. Do you issue binding advance rulings on a) classification b) value?
26. Can challenges to Customs decisions be referred to an outside, neutral tribunal?
27. Are Customs agents licensed? Do they have a monopoly?
28. Do you have a training school? If so, what subjects are covered?
29. Are any Customs functions currently handled by private agencies? If so, which? What is your experience of these arrangements?
30. What are normal working hours? Is Customs attendance available outside working hours and, if so, on what basis of compensation?

Preshipment Inspection Agency

Thirty or more governments have passed certain Customs functions—typically valuation—to specialist private enterprise agencies. These companies are usually required to carry out quality inspection of cargoes/consignments at overseas points of export.

This move was highly innovative at a time, some thirty years ago, when exchange difficulties, for many countries, were exacerbated by capital flight frequently aided by fraudulent invoices. It also helped countries, which came to sudden affluence with the spectacular rise in oil prices some years later, to limit the extent to which they were exploited by foreign suppliers.

More recently the main advantage has been in the reduction of revenue losses attributable to inefficient/dishonest Customs.

Unfortunately the system, in its general features and management, has hardly altered since its inception, and has now acquired some of the weaknesses that it is intended to overcome in Customs administrations.

There is, for example, no known attempt by any of these agencies to apply modern risk-assessment techniques to limit the scope of their physical inspections. Apart from the formal appeal system set up by the WTO to meet user complaints, there is no effective mechanism for regular consultation with traders and carriers affected by pre-shipment controls.

At the moment PSI activities cause extra delays and associated costs to traders, carriers and ultimately their customers.

When looking at these operations it is useful to know whether more than one company is providing the PSI service and on what basis any choice is made—for example by the importer or, geographically, according to the country of origin of the goods.

Questions

1. How many Reports of Findings do you issue annually? What is the value of the consignments covered by these Reports?
2. What is the average time taken to issue a Report?
3. What goods are excluded from PSI and what is the minimum value under which PSI does not apply?
4. What proportion of consignments are physically inspected?
5. On what basis do you charge and secure payment for these inspections?
6. What is the basis of your central, contractual remuneration?
7. Do you apply/are you planning to apply, any risk-assessment techniques to reduce the incidence of physical inspection? If so, on what broad lines and by what methods?
8. Do you supply training services to the Customs? If so, on what subjects and how is the quality of the training assessed?
9. Do you exchange data electronically? If so with whom?
10. Do you use a) the Internet b) satellite communication? If so for what purposes?

Chamber of Commerce

Some explanation of the extent and duration of facilitation problems can often be found in the absence of any organized means of identifying and defining difficulties and proposing and promoting relevant solutions.

Facilitation is handicapped in many important respects. In many businesses it is still seen as a matter for the shipping office, itself a low-profile management concern. It has no single, perceptible obstacle to present at the policy level, only a rag-bag of tangled details straying over Customs, banks, transport, insurance and such awkward extras as dangerous goods, illicit drugs and security.

In advanced economies many of these difficulties are being ironed out by the radical review of practice and procedure implicit in and imposed by computerization linked to an increasingly powerful and accessible range of associated new technologies.

This situation puts justified emphasis on institutions within which notes can be compared, outline information on technology transferred, joint analysis undertaken and common policies agreed and supported.

The preferred institutional focus, thought up, applied and in many cases now discarded, by developed countries, is a special national facilitation committee, under direct government patronage. This has some early superficial advantages, but can often raise as many problems as it is intended to solve. One immediate question is the status of Customs. If they are put in charge progress may be slow. If some other agency is in command then Customs will, almost automatically, be highly reserved.

Another difficulty is the cost of a new, separate secretariat and the very likely shortage of any suitable manager.

These and other associated issues may take months to resolve, while the central analytical Report on which most such institutions are based, may become progressively out of date and unfashionable. One initial step, which may develop into a satisfactory long-term solution, but which can, in any event, present few tangible disadvantages, is to use the best available Chamber of Commerce as a sort of institutional kangaroo pouch.

This gives the Chamber an extra, practical activity, that can widen and deepen its existing interface with outside third parties, including Customs and could, at some points in a practical work program, offer useful income from publications and conferences.

The Chamber formula is preferable to such an alternative source of support as a national export promotion agency because this, by definition, will give priority to exports—while the main facilitation obstacles operate at import—and often consist largely of manufacturing industry representatives, with little concern for detailed transport, payment, and Customs procedures.

It should be noted that Chambers are also participants in the procedural chain insofar as they issue Certificates of Origin and may take part in the ATA Carnet system.

Chambers tend, especially in Francophone countries, to have strong links to their counterparts in developed economies, which can be very valuable in supporting contacts and cooperation with outside, often international, interests, which have every practical incentive to help facilitation work worldwide.

Some assessment of the general status and efficiency of a Chamber will be a relevant part of any worth-while facilitation audit

Questions

1. What is your membership? Is this statutory or on a voluntary basis?
2. Do you offer advice to exporters and importers on:
   - National and foreign Customs requirements?
   - Foreign standards, dangerous goods regulations, and so on?
   - Payment systems, including documentary credits?
   - Containerized, multimodal transport?
3. Do you have specialist committees for questions related to:
   - Customs?
   - Commercial banking?
   - Transport?
   - Communications?
   - Electronic commerce?
4. Do you run courses on any of these subjects? If so, which?
5. Are you in touch with:
   - The National Committee of the International Chamber of Commerce (ICC)?
   - The ICC itself?
   - The International Bureau of Chambers of Commerce?
   - The UNCTAD/WTO International Trade Center?
   - Any overseas Chambers? If so which?
   - Any regional inter-governmental bodies, for example, APEC, MERCOSUR, EU?
6. Do you issue Certificates of Origin? If so, how many annually? Do you verify what you certify? If so, how?
7. Do you participate in the ATA carnet system? How many transactions do you deal with annually and do you experience any difficulties in this work?
8. Do you have formal consultative arrangements with Customs? If so, on what subjects?
9. Do you consult/collaborate with other national business organizations on any aspect of international trade. If so, which and on what subjects?

Department of Trade and Industry

This heading would also include any hived-off Foreign Trade agency.

While these Departments are often lower in the domestic bureaucratic pecking-order than Customs, which usually enjoys strong links to the Ministry of Finance, they have gained a new international status through the growing scope and authority of the World Trade Organization.

This has special significance for trade facilitation policy because there is a strong likelihood that the subject will be raised for consideration in the next WTO negotiating round. Even if this does not happen, commercial pressures for WTO attention to key facilitation problems are hardening and the whole facilitation concept is almost certain to graduate from small print to headlines in the trade and financial press for many months to come.

The results of a balanced facilitation audit, reflected in an analytical report, with recommendations for action, could be very useful to Trade Ministers in this situation and be a useful means of focusing attention and perhaps support on a number of urgent reforms.

This Questionnaire is not so much a means of acquiring information as an indirect effort to impart it.

Questions

1. What are the main items making up a) exports b) imports in a recent typical year?

2. Do you have any existing focus for dealing with such trade facilitation tasks as the simplification and standardization of documents and formalities, the shift from paper to electronic commerce and the revision of the national regulatory framework affecting goods in international movement? If so, of what sort and with what objectives?
3. Are you aware of or active in current WTO inquiries into the nature and needs of international trade facilitation?
4. Is the Department able to offer rapid, efficient Customs clearance of goods as an inducement to overseas companies considering direct inward investment in manufacturing?
5. How far does the Department consult small and medium-size companies on the extent to which their overseas trading performance and prospects are affected by Customs and other import/export formalities?
6. Does the Department monitor and review the operation of payment systems, including, particularly, documentary credits, as possible constraints on national performance in world markets?
7. Is the Department aware of, and, if so, does it take part in any of the many regional activities—for example ASEAN, APEC, MERCOSUR, SADC, EU—now supporting practical trade facilitation work programs?
8. Has the Department studied the need for safe, timely and reliable delivery services in relation to export performance? If so, are traders able to use postal, express carrier, containerized through transport services and roll-on/roll-off road services freely and to full effect?
9. Is the Department bringing electronic commerce practices and technology to the attention of traders and carriers and assisting them to identify particularly relevant possibilities and developments?
10. Is there a national standards institution? If so, does it advise exporters on the foreign standard requirements? If not who does this?
11. Do you generate timely and accurate statistics on trade flows? Are these collected by Customs by requiring relevant information at export? If so, have you considered alternative, non-interventionist methods, for example sampling?

Analysis and Interpretation

This will normally take the form of an Audit Report, structured around the main interacting themes of Customs, payment, transport, port, airport, exchange control and pre-shipment inspection procedures.

This report would be written by the person(s) responsible for the interviews. If Audits of this sort are likely to be regular activity then it would be worthwhile to get some experienced consultancy advice on the first Report.

Experience has shown, however, that familiarity with the process of questioning and reporting grows very rapidly, which suggests that anyone who has acquired an initial experience should be seen as a preferred candidate for other Audits elsewhere.

The main purpose of the Audit report should be to identify and describe the problems, their operational inter-relationship and existing institutional background.

The Report would include recommendations for remedial action. These should be presented as provisional and seen as a focus for more detailed "democratic" examination and discussion among the main interested parties.

Remedial Action

The Report, possibly edited to reduce the more critical passages, should be circulated to:

- All those interviewed.
- All relevant government Departments, official agencies, trade associations, including resident foreign Chambers of Commerce and the trade and financial press.
- Any regional economic grouping which might have a direct interest in the country concerned.

The Report should also be sent, for information, to persons responsible for facilitation policy in selected international bodies, including the WTO, ICC, WCO, IATA, FIATA, ICS, IRU and IBCC.

Opportunities should be provided for an initial discussion, in the country concerned, among those most directly concerned by its assessments and recommendations.

This should be followed, reasonably quickly, by an open Seminar/Workshop.

Once the Report has been amended as necessary and validated, it should be the basis of an Action Plan and Management Project.

The Action Plan will require:

- A full assessment of justification and risks.
- A detailed set of deliverables and associated timetables.
- Proposals for institution building and support.
- Specific descriptions of any additional in-depth studies.
- Plan cost estimates.

The initial Report will leave many issues for later, more detailed study. In particular, the Report should identify those facilitation difficulties that need, and would be suitable for, measurement and costing.

Project costings will depend not only on what needs to be done but on what funding is likely to be available.

A major problem is to identify necessary outside expertise. There are many experts available in Customs, transport, banking, or port or trade association management, but very few, indeed, can deal with any one of these subjects in depth, with an experienced eye on its full, operational relationship to the rest, within a comprehensive facilitation program.

Identifying such experts, drafting their Terms of Reference, fixing the sequence and/or combination in which they should work, and monitoring and assembling their findings, will be a complex professional task.

It will be best confided, on a part-time basis, to a consultant or in-house Project Manager, responsible for all stages of what will usually prove at least a two-year initial work program.

Ideally, the Project should include a full-time on-site expert, to set in place and assist the basic institutional mechanisms, guide early consultations and activities, give informal training to local staff and generally keep all the main work items moving forward to timetable.

All these stages, following the Audit and initial Report, could provide very interesting opportunities for specialized private sector agencies to develop relevant project management skills and, possibly even more important, to locate, assemble and maintain a core of inter-related supporting expertise.